CONTENTS

INTRODUCTION

Lilian Lucy Davidson (1879–1954) painted the emotively expressionist work *Gorta* (Famine) in 1946 **[Figure 2]**. The painting was formerly known as *Burying the Child*. The wretchedness of the figures, the burnt grass, the image's shadowy tones and cheerless palette reflect on the grim scenario depicted. A tiny bundle of an infant prematurely dead from Famine is wrapped in a brown woolen blanket, and is about to be buried. The grief-stricken family have created a grave in open countryside. There is no cemetery or plot marker; the place is unremarkable; perhaps it is the site of a *cillín*, an unconsecrated burial ground for unbaptized children and people on society's margins. For this child there is no ceremonial shroud, no mourning neighbors, no keeners, no gravediggers.

During the worst of the Famine years, graves were dug in various and some unlikely places across the landscape of Ireland as mortality rates rose. What were known as paupers' plots in cemeteries, together with other graveyards of the impoverished who had the misfortune to die in workhouses built from the 1830s, became Famine burial pits. These gravesites were typically located at the edge of formal cemeteries, near workhouses, or on the outskirts of towns and villages across Ireland. There was little to no demarcation as to where individuals were buried, or even a common headstone listing their names. As the pace of deaths from starvation-related illnesses increased, these sites, and other hurriedly allotted Famine plots, were marked by repeatedly turned earth to become graves upon graves, some interring hundreds of the Famine dead.

As suggested by Davidson's image, many did not even reach such grim communal sites, but were buried alone and in passing at roadsides and in fields. In such instances surviving family members or neighbors sought to bury the dead in haste, fearing contagion from the corpse or in order to attempt survival by moving on in search of relief aid or the possibility of emigration.

In *Gorta* the figurative distortions, reduced palette, and emphasis on the anguish of the gravediggers are heightened by the pathetic fallacy of the looming dark, arched cloud formation. These pictorial elements both intensify the raw human drama

Figure 2 | Lilian Lucy Davidson, *Gorta*

of such a burial scene and signpost the anguished days ahead for the temporary survivors depicted. The painting is in stark counterpoint to Davidson's colorful genre scenes of markets and fairs in Ireland, and followed on from what Katherine Cahill terms her "Western peasant cycle of paintings" of the 1920s and 1930s (36).[1] As a "journeyman artist", Davidson earned her living through sales, commissions, teaching, and her writing, which Cahill suggests fostered the artist's defining "empathy with her subjects" (36).

Gorta reflects Davidson's absorption of stylistic developments in international art practice, as well as her interest in Irish genre subjects. It was exhibited during the centenary era of the Famine in 1946 in the *Exhibition of Pictures of Irish Historical Interest* at the National College of Art and Design in Dublin. Organised in connection with the centenary commemoration of Thomas Davis and the Young Ireland movement, this was the first significant commemorative exhibition to include art on the subject of the Famine. The event, however, was predominantly concerned with a celebratory tone, as it was organized on the theme of Irish political freedom. The few works that depicted the Famine were in the open-submission section, while the larger part of the exhibition was comprised of works loaned from national and municipal collections in Dublin. Many of these were portraits of celebrated figures associated with Ireland's emancipation, and heroic scenes of the liberation of the country from its former imperial ruler, Britain.

A brave and overtly emotive submission to the 1946 exhibition was Davidson's *Gorta* – then, as now, a retrospective image, the visual statement of an artist looking back at a subject outside of her experience. The makers and promoters of many forms of commemorative visual culture and practices similarly seek to create forms of secondary witnessing, to borrow Dora Apel's phrase. This is evident in analyses of memorial cultures of grievous histories, including, notably, literature on the memory of holocausts, such as that during the Second World War.[2] Writing about what it is to bear direct witness to events and experiences considered radically indescribable, such as those in Second World War concentration camps, Giorgio Agamben accounts the "ultimate witnesses" as those that can never speak of what they experienced: including the dead.

Oscillating discourses in cultural theory on concepts of post-memory and vicarious pasts attest, simultaneously, to the limits on knowledge and breadth of desire to remember the experiences of others who have gone before. Marianne Hirsch's ideas of post-memory offer a means of recall for events not directly experienced by the subject in their lifetime, often triggered by an image or object of, often parental, association. In a related context, James Young has described "vicarious pasts": "by calling attention to their vicarious relationship to events, the next generation ensures that their 'post-memory' of events remains an unfinished, ephemeral process, not a means towards a definitive answer to impossible questions" (2). By contrast, David Rieff contends that only an individual is capable of memory, and his polemical call for acts of forgetting as a moral counterpoint to problematic myth-making, or "'constructed' collective memory ... anodyne to the culture of grievance" (13), illustrates the potent complexity of nuanced historical knowledge. Such "constructed" memory, for Rieff, can be linked to treacherously composed rhetoric of nationalistic collective remembrances. After-images, then, are in the first iteration portrayals of a grievous history produced by the children of survivors of that event, and can be usefully recognized, like all moments of representation, as beginning at a remove from the event referenced.

In the course of the Irish Famine, suffering unto death became a dreadful spectacle for others to recount. A range of contemporary observers – including news writers and illustrators, Poor Law inspectors, doctors, philanthropists, and visitors to the country – not only wrote but also published accounts of their experiences. Quality of life and of death during the Famine can be gleaned from statistical records, such as census information before and after the Famine, workhouse records, and emigration and shipping logs. But it is the information gathered by the National Folklore Collection (NFC) (initially known as the Irish Folklore Commission, 1934–71) that provides insight into the culturally complex aspects of both dying and subsequent mortuary practices before, during, and after the Famine. This archive's "oral narratives", to use Niall Ó Ciosáin's term (222), are the memories of mostly elderly informants who had a vicarious sense of this history given their generational closeness to the events of the 1840s.

The mostly land-laboring families of Ireland at the time – numbering around 300,000 cottier households and over 600,000 laborer households (Ó Murchadha 4–7) – suffered the brunt of the Famine. Some were tenants of landlords with large estates. Many were disastrously dependent on conacre farming – renting tiny plots for the growing season and cultivating potatoes as a central diet (Ó Murchadha 4–7). Over two thirds of the labor force depended on agriculture; the majority of these held little or no land, and traded "their labor for a small plot of land" (Kinealy 18). Such materially impoverished living conditions are pictured in (Henry) Mark Anthony's elegiac tondo image from the 1840s, *Sunset (View of the Rock of Cashel from the Village)* [Cover].

Collectively, such households made up more than three million of the over eight million population recorded in the 1841 census (Stephen J. Campbell 15). On the eve of the Famine, in early 1845, the population may well have been close to 8.5 million (Bartlett 281). In the following ten years, as a widely estimated two million emigrated, 1.1 million died in Ireland from hunger and related diseases. Their troubled passing and progressively cursory interment demonstrated the extent of their catastrophic social, economic, and political vulnerability.

Looking to the scrupulous formulations of pre-Famine traditions – the ritualized display of the corpse followed by intricate obsequies – we can see just how far much of the Irish population had traveled from their careful vigilance over the dying as traumatic situations of torturous and grotesque death forcibly transformed parts of the landscape of Ireland into a bleak landscape of unintended gravesites. The significance of the rural Irish cottiers' and land-workers' pre-Famine mortuary rituals are pictorially recounted in paintings and illustrations from the eighteenth and nineteenth centuries. Then – as more recently – cultural customs around death, burial, and mourning were intrinsic to both the formations of individual recall and constructed notions of collective memory, such as cultural memory, which Ann Rigney notes as "the product of representations" (15) and "always a form of vicarious memory" (25). She writes: "The term 'cultural memory' highlights the extent to which shared memories of the past are the product of mediation, textualization, and acts of communication" (14). As Elizabeth Hallam and Jenny Hockey note,

The social experiences of dying and death, together with memory processes that are activated in relation to them, are therefore enmeshed in wider political, religious and intellectual factors. These influence or sustain (or, conversely, work to erode) solitary as well as collective remembering so that we need to attend to the individual body and its relation to the social body in the act of making memory (16).

PRE-FAMINE "ASSEMBLY CUSTOMS" AND THE MERRY WAKE

In vivid contrast to the overwhelming familial desolation and social isolation suggested by Davidson's Famine image, pre-Famine paintings on the subject of bodies post-mortem demonstrate what Gearóid Ó Crualaoich has termed "assembly custom" (191) as a definitive aspect of Irish mortuary traditions. The continuance of the customary social gatherings in the face of sharp and repeated disapproval from religious and civil institutions and authorities, recorded as early as 1614 (174), was, Ó Crualaoich argues, a type of "resistance" to these controlling forces (173). The criticisms usually focused on the apparent excessive preparatory and hospitality costs, and on presumed impropriety of the livelier aspects of the merrymaking and consumption of alcohol at wakes. Pre-Famine mortuary and funerary practices integrated religious and pre-Christian, that is to say pagan and Celtic, traditions. The rituals were highly organized, social, and symbolic events that marked at once the passing of one life into the next world and the endurance of the community. Greatly thwarted by the Famine and its devastating fall-outs – firstly demographic and consequently cultural – mortuary customs were somewhat revitalized in late decades of the nineteenth century and into the early twentieth century. Even so, others felt changing social values in a post-Famine landscape implied wake conventions lacked respectability (Lysaght, "Hospitality" 417), and eventually more religious forms dominated Irish mortuary practices.

A wake, as depicted in *The Wake*, c. 1783, by Cork painter Nathaniel Grogan the Elder (1739/40–1807), occurred after the laying out of the body, which was generally a private affair, and before the funeral and burial of the deceased [Figure 3]. In this painting the corpse is depicted laid out and dressed in a white shroud. Habits or special dress were also used in some regions. The strategic arranging of white sheets, as shown, was common in the laying-out ritual (Ó Crualaoich 180), as was the setting of candles near the corpse (Kinmonth 166). Such sheets were typically stored for the purposes of wakes and utilized across a given community (Ó Crualaoich 180). After the body of the deceased had been left for a time – sometimes with big toes tied together until the body was cold (Ó Crualaoich 181) – then washed and dressed, it was usually laid out on a prominent piece of furniture, such as a kitchen table. The positioning of a corpse at a wake indicated their role as "host of the occasion" (Lysaght, "Hospitality" 419).

Figure 3 | Nathaniel Grogan the Elder, *The Wake*

A wake began when wider family and community gathered to celebrate and mourn the deceased, and it usually continued over at least two nights (Ó Súilleabháin 53–4). This gave mourners a chance to travel from other townlands, with overnight vigils implicit in the name, "wake" being the translation of the Gaelic terms *tórramh* (funeral or gathering) or *faire* (vigil). Grogan's painted wake is in a barn-like space with domestic trappings, as noted by Claudia Kinmonth (165). This reflects on the extent of the social occasion: the home of the deceased was a preferable location, but if the crowd proved too large, a nearby larger building was used. The formation of the group in the foreground, the welcome implied by the roaring fire on the right, and a woman smoking a clay pipe on the left of the scene are suggestive of the expected atmosphere of merriment and social entertainment at wakes.

Though Grogan was primarily a landscape artist (Dunne 8), Tom Dunne observes that the relative scarcity of Irish genre pictures, when compared to contemporary England, makes the genre element of Grogan's *oeuvre* all the more valuable (88).[3] Nicola Figgis suggests that "For Grogan the representation of character and the injection of humour were more important considerations" (277) than academic practice. The license of gentle humor is apparent in this work, in particular with Grogan's attention to the semi-circular group in the foreground – with a figure in the center – whose formation suggests some of the social games played at wakes. A "borekeen" was a master of merriment who organized interactive games – some with pagan origin – storytelling, and even tricks or pranks. Grogan's image may be a depiction of a game similar to the "brogue about". In this an old shoe is passed around a circular group of men on the floor, under raised knees. As a person in the middle of the group tries to find it, they are hit on the back with the shoe (Ó Crualaoich 186).

While a number of games pitted group against group, many involved an individual targeted by a group. Ó Súilleabháin recounts witnessing "croosting" (66), which consisted of the throwing of pieces of turf – or whatever was to hand, such as potatoes or clay pipes broken for the purpose – generally in the direction of a cranky individual. Other games incorporated "set pieces", as described by Ó Crualaoich, such as men forming a human pyramid, with the highest man left dangling from a roof's cross-beam as those below run off (185). This type of horseplay extended to a variety of high-spirited games that had potential to, and sometimes did, result in actual combat, and, on occasion, even led to faction fighting. The range of pranks played were considerable, from pepper mixed into shared pipe tobacco resulting in sneezing mourners, or the tying of bootlaces of individuals sitting beside each other, to leaving a player who had been blindfolded during a game alone with the corpse in the house (Ó Súilleabháin 67).

Though the more boisterous pranks and games were largely the domain of men, facilitated by the borekeen, other set games included both men and women, and took the form of satirical play, commonly mocking various institutions of the Church, such as marriage. Dancing and courting between the sexes was also common, as was matchmaking. The effusive tone and raucous nature of these activities were implicated in the Church's regular condemnation of wakes, leading to the issuing over a period of three hundred years of edicts aimed at suppressing such traditions (Ó Súilleabháin *passim*). Patricia Lysaght argues that the more licentious games were "concerned, on a symbolic level, with the perpetuation of the life of the community" ("Hospitality" 419).

The family of the deceased provided what food and drink they could afford, such as meat, bread, whiskey, and brandy, with plates of snuff and "bodhrán-fuls of clay pipes" also offered to mourners (Ó Crualaoich 184). At wakes in County Galway the pipes were known as "Lord ha mercies" (Ó Crualaoich 187), an abbreviation of a common blessing for the deceased: May the Lord have mercy on his/her soul. The hospitality provided was considered "commensurate with the deceased's social position" (Lysaght, "Hospitality" 407), and was intended to maintain the family's position and "merit the good will and respect of the neighbours" (Lysaght, "Hospitality" 407). As a culturally crucial part of the process of mourning, wakes were prepared for years in advance, with laying-out and burial garments sought out and paid for, even ahead of day-to-day clothing needs (Ó Crualaoich 174; Lysaght, "Hospitality" 405). Religious components were also key to pre-Famine mortuary rites: blessings and prayers, including the rosary and *de profundis*, were recited; rosary beads intertwined the fingers of the corpse, and a funeral Mass was said before the burial.

In the background of Grogan's painting, the old women by the corpse may well be depictions of keeners – or cryers – who, along with family members, cried at strategic moments. The term "keen" is an anglicized version of the Gaelic word for crying, *caoineadh*. Customarily, the family of the deceased would keen at the beginning of a wake. Women who regularly keened at wakes would then sustain the keening and lamentations at intervals throughout the night. This practice greatly intensified the emotional pitch of the event (Lysaght, "Caoineadh" 74), but could also result in competitive keening, which in turn could occasionally lead to a humorous spectacle of keeners insulting each other (Lysaght, "Caoineadh" 71).

Keeners were paid with food or "whiskey or tobacco or a few shillings" (Ó Coileáin 107). Angela Bourke notes that for professional keeners, usually older women "experienced in loss and grief", it was their sole means of support ("Inner lives" 15). Their lamentations were metrically defined and drew on formulae of lament poetry. Some have survived, with intervention and revision, as poems celebrating the lives of heroic figures, such as the epic *Lament for Art O'Leary*.[4] Described by Bourke as "elaborate verbal art" ("Inner lives" 16), the textual content of performed laments were not only centered on the dead but expanded upon a range of topics regarding the company present, their history and conduct ("Inner lives" 14, 16). Seán Ó Coileáin notes that the decline of keening through the nineteenth century was in large part due to pressure from the Church, which considered it, along with other

Figure 4 | Frederic William Burton, *The Aran Fisherman's Drowned Child*

wake practices, to be abhorrent (115). He acknowledges that the Famine hastened this process, as "the social significance of death, the need and opportunity to mark it off" were lost (115).

As agents of "mournful transition" for the dead from one life to another (Ó Crualaoich 192), keeners were integral to the mourning process at both wakes and burials. In Frederic William Burton's (1816–1900) watercolor painting *The Aran Fisherman's Drowned Child* (1841), the tragedy of the sudden passing of the young child is stated not only with the despairing demeanors of the family but by the dramatic gestures of the keening woman lamenting the dead child **[Figure 4]**.[5] Already, the community has gathered and the shawled women at the door have the appearance of keeners.

At a wake following an unexpected or tragic death, such as depicted by Burton, a more somber tone would prevail than that following the death of an elderly person deemed to have lived a full life. Unexpected deaths were often attributed to the fairies, and were mourned with greater superstition. Superstitions about fairies and or supposed supernatural phenomena manifested across the spectrum of mortuary and mourning practices, from harbingers of death to the burial of the corpse. For example, the banshee was thought to be a female supernatural death-messenger whose cry foretold a death. "Banshee" is the anglicized form of the Irish *bean-sidhe*, meaning "woman of the fairies" – as Lysaght phrases it, "otherworld woman" ("Banshee" 158), whose non-verbal cry is "loud, plaintive and intensely lonesome" ("Banshee" 159). In some cases the fairies were said to leave signs predicting a death, or a death-tick could be "heard" in the walls or furniture of a house when a death was imminent. Fairy keening heard during a wake was not considered frightening as it suggested an expression of respect for the dead from the so-called "other side" (Ó Crualaoich 178). It was also widely considered unlucky to leave a wake alone or between midnight and daybreak, as spirits – of both the fairies and the dead – were thought to be active.

According to Bourke, fairy legends reflected on societal anxiety around fertility (*Burning of Bridget Cleary* 36) and circumstances of mortality, such as childbirth, which were related by stories of women swept through the air (*Burning of Bridget Cleary* 37). Difficult behavior – in infants in particular – and mental illnesses were theorized through tales of changelings and fairy abductions (*Burning of Bridget Cleary* 4, 30). Timothy Corrigan Correll outlines how "belief in fairies and folk healers existed in a dialectical relationship with disbelief" (14), and notes that discussions centered on supernatural or magical forces were a feature of fireside storytelling at wakes and other night-time rural gatherings (3). The archive of the NFC includes wide variations of these stories of contestation, and, as Bourke notes, fairy legends were linked to notable aspects of known landscapes (*Burning of Bridget Cleary* 8).

The Aran Fisherman's Drowned Child brought Burton much public acclaim as a young artist, and was the most popular print ever reproduced by the Royal Irish Art Union (Marie Bourke 7). Born in Corofin, County Clare, Burton's empathy with the scene is clear in the emotional mood of the depiction and his attention to contemporary detail. Though Brian Kennedy writes that Burton visited the Aran Islands several times between 1838 and 1841 with the antiquarian George Petrie (23), Marie Bourke suggests the work was first modeled in the Claddagh in Galway and later completed in Dublin (cited in Kinmonth 168). He made over fifty studies for this studio painting, and modeled the figures on relatives and friends (Marie Bourke 7). Brian P. Kennedy observes that Burton's use of watercolors was so controlled that his works have the initial appearance of oil paintings (23), which might be explained by the extensive preparatory work. The details of the clothing are accurately observed for the period, and the domestic setting gives a good sense of the interior of single-roomed mud-built cottages of the Famine era.

At a time when the British art establishment tended toward either sentiment or outright pictorial mockery of Irish customs, sincere observation of Irish social life and mores was central to the work of another young Irish artist: painter and illustrator, Cork-born Daniel Macdonald (1821–53). He was twenty-one and living in Cork city when he made the drawing *Returning from an Irish Funeral* **[Figure 5]**.[6] Niamh O'Sullivan draws attention to "the humour and jollity of carnivalesque aspects of everyday life" in the image (*In the Lion's Den* 70). The atmosphere is lively, as funeral-goers and gravediggers ride home on the small, covered, two-wheeled, horse-drawn cart. While the scene's pictorial silhouette is imbued with the culturally symbolic markers of a round tower and ruined church, it also documents a bare-footed boy, pigs, geese, and a dog, and a rough terrain as a road. Life goes on, as the graveyard is barely visible in the background.

Commonly, on removal from the wake house, the coffin was laid down on chairs outside the home of the deceased for a few moments. The routes taken to a grave were often inclusive of symbolic stops, which reflected on a range of social complexities. These decisions were dependent on the type of death that had taken place and on inter-familial relations within the community, as well as on superstitions associated with the death. The digging of the grave and physical burial of the body were also symbolically and sometimes superstitiously devised, with regional variation regarding how and by whom these were conducted. It is reported, for example, that in County Galway, so as to avoid fairies and bad luck, a coffin was never left down on its way to the grave (Ó Crualaoich 190), and in County Cork two shovels were left crossed on a dug grave to prevent spirit or fairy intervention before burial (Ó Crualaoich 188). While a funeral Mass or prayers usually took place at the house of the deceased or sometimes at a nearby church, the burial itself was often conducted without a priest.

Figure 5 | Daniel Macdonald, *Returning from an Irish Funeral*

Macdonald's image highlights the social nature of pre-Famine obsequies, where private loss was transformed, through variously enacted mortuary and funerary customs, into a public and shared form of mourning. The "social cathartic chaos out of which a new social order can emerge" (Ó Crualaoich 191) was implied in the robustly vivacious aspects of Irish mourning games, and is here suggested by the exuberance of this fast-moving and unruly post-funeral cortège.

Within a shockingly short period of time, as the Famine and its far-reaching effects transpired, such meaningful cultural practices around death were impossible, and the act of dying itself was depleted of its capacity for signifying social dignity.

Figure 6 | Muriel Brandt, *An Gorta* [Detail]

"THEY WERE BURIED WHERE THEY WERE FOUND [...] DEATH MOWED A WIDE SWATH": DEATH AND BURIAL DURING THE FAMINE

The focal point of the composition in Muriel Brandt's (1909–81) *An Gorta* (c. 1946) is a woman surrounded by children **[Figure 6, detail]**. In the middle ground a group of people are carrying a sealed coffin, implying a funeral procession **[Figure 1, full image, pp 4–5]**.[7] As in Davidson's image, the ground underfoot is arid, and background mountainous contours echo an Irish topography. Brandt's work was also exhibited at the 1946 *Exhibition of Pictures of Irish Historical Interest*. In light of the artistic climate of the time – divided between academy traditions (such as the Royal Hibernian Academy) and artists who supported the more modern Exhibitions of Living Art (ELA) (spearheaded in 1943 by Irish artist Mainie Jellett) – the 1946 exhibition was academically aligned with heroic history subjects and portrait art. Within that context Davidson's and Brandt's paintings contributed to a burgeoning set of after-images of the Famine as they forcibly relocated the conventional subjects of genre art into a decidedly unheroic form of history painting.

Brandt's densely populated canvas is in keeping with her rural and urban scenes, though it belies the extent to which conventions surrounding death and burial were fast disappearing as the Famine progressed. Well regarded for her paintings of children,[8] Brandt renders them here with careful attention. The clothing of the figures throughout suggests the artist's interest in traditional clothing, including a black hooded cape, red skirts, and shawls worn by the woman and breeches by the men. The mournful tone of the work is extended to both the dead – epitomized by the coffin and its bearers – and the doomed prospects of the living, achieved by the apparent dejection and exhaustion of the foregrounded group.

The mournful tone of the small crowd and serenity of the scene presented in Cork-born James Mahony's "Funeral at Shepperton Lakes" **[Figure 7]** is evocatively poignant when compared to the lively social nature of pre-Famine mortuary traditions, as imaged by Grogan. A series of images was published in the *Illustrated London News* (*ILN*) on February 13, 1847 in the context of Mahony's written report:

After leaving Clonakilty, each step that we took westward brought fresh evidence of the truth of the reports of the misery, as we either met a funeral or a coffin at every hundred yards, until we approached the country of the Shepperton Lakes ... Here, the distress became more striking, from the decrease of numbers at the funerals, none having more than eight or ten attendants, and many only two or three.

Mahony also drew "Mullins' Hut at Scull", printed in the *ILN* on February 20, 1847 – one of just two illustrations of dying Famine victims published in the *ILN*; the other was "Sketch in a House at Fahy's Quay, Ennis – The Widow Connor and her Dying Child", published on January 5, 1850. Each was accompanied by a written report affectively describing the pitiful conditions encountered.[9]

As people were dying and displaced on a rapidly rising scale, burials became increasingly hasty, with ever more rudimentary methods of burial allowing little possibility for the structured community gatherings of earlier mortuary customs. Coffins became difficult to attain, becoming relatively expensive and increasingly rare. Some used furniture to make home-made coffins. Common coffins, also known as hinged coffins, were used at some graveyards and workhouse burial sites: the base was opened and the body dropped to the earth so that the coffin could be reused (Póirtéir 8), as described here:

During the frightful plague, which devastated a large proportion of Ireland in the years 1846–47 – that monstrous and unChristian machine a "sliding coffin" was from necessity used in Bantry Union for the conveyance of the victims to one common grave. The material of this cross, the symbol of our Redemption, is a portion of one of the machines, which enclosed the remains of several hundreds of our countrymen during their passage from the wretched huts or waysides where they died, to the pit, into which their remains were thrown. T.W.

This text is reputed to have been written by Dr Thomas Willis and pasted onto the back of the bottom shaft of one of three crosses he is thought to have fashioned from the base of a hinged coffin (O'Rourke 3) **[Figure 8]**. Also on the back of this cross is paper with the text: "This Cross was given to me about the year 1870 by Thos Willis MD then residing at Rathmines, Maynooth 3rd June 1885, John O'Rourke". Canon John O'Rourke added a metal figure of Jesus to the front of the cross. He subsequently donated it to the Presentation Sisters in Maynooth, County Kildare, and it is now on display in the atrium of Mount St Anne's Retreat and Conference Centre, Killenard, Portarlington, County Laois.

Willis was a Dublin-based physician and apothecary best known for his promotion of the health of the working classes, and was a founding member of the Irish St Vincent de Paul charity in 1844. He was appointed one of two Poor Law inspectors for Bantry, County Cork in 1847 after serving as a guardian of the Bantry workhouse (Martin 71). There Willis witnessed the inadequacies of relief systems. While Bantry workhouse was originally built to accommodate six hundred (O'Connor 234), it

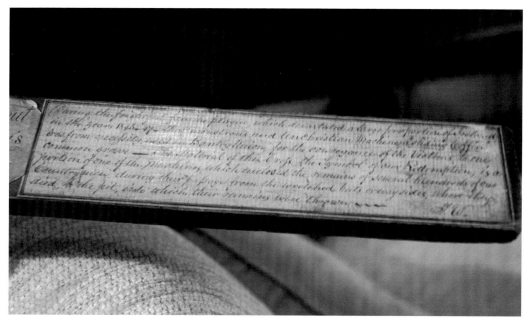

Figure 8 | Text reportedly written by Dr Thomas Willis on Famine-era coffin cross

became clearly overburdened: workhouse minutes of May 5, 1849 note an aspiration to reduce the number of inmates to eighteen hundred by the following week (Martin 147). During Willis's time there the workhouse opened extensions and auxiliary sites intended to accommodate 976 inmates (Martin 147), but remained unable to cope with the scale of the unfolding catastrophe.

In many places, workhouses were overwhelmed by the scale and spread of infections, as Laurence M. Geary comments:

While mismanagement and negligence were a feature of some institutions and while the conditions in many were appalling, it would be wrong to attach the entire blame to administrative indifference. The system was simply unable to cope with the demands made upon it by the Famine (56).

Dr Daniel Donovan described the outwardly physical signs of some diseases arising from severe starvation and the speed with which such suffering bodies deteriorated at this terrible time. Based in Skibbereen, County Cork, he administered tirelessly to the sick and dying during the Famine, and also worked to aid emigration (Foynes 54–5). In 1848 he had an article on this subject published in the *Dublin Medical Press*:

In a short time the face and limbs become frightfully emaciated; the eyes acquire a most peculiar stare; the skin exhaled a peculiar and offensive foetor, and was covered with a brownish filthy-looking coating, almost as indelible as varnish. This I was at first inclined to regard as encrusted filth, but further experience has convinced me that this is a secretion poured out from the exhalants on the surface of the body (qtd. in Crawford 200–1).

As starvation leads to severe vitamin deficiencies, the susceptibility of Famine victims, generally, to epidemics and related fevers, as well as more ordinarily avoidable conditions, such as scurvy, pellagra, and eye diseases, greatly increases (Crawford 205). Margaret Crawford notes that the externally recognizable signs of nutritional deprivation in children include marasmus, which is visible in the shrunken frames marked with premature aging, and kwashiorkor, notable for oedema in the stomach and lower limbs (198). As these illness advance they give rise to browned pigmentation of the skin and the appearance of downy facial (lanugo) hair, similar to that described by Donovan.

Geary outlines how the impairment of an individual's immune system by starvation in tandem with the loss of community resistance to the spread of disease facilitated the occurrence of epidemics (49). He notes that so-called Famine fever in 1840s Ireland was usually related to typhus fever and relapsing fever (49). He lists fever, dysentery, and smallpox as causing "terrifying mortality" during the Famine, along with tuberculosis, rheumatic fever, bronchitis, influenza, pneumonia, diarrhea, and measles, with an added pandemic of Asiatic cholera in 1848–49 worsening an already drastic situation (49). This all impacted upon the subsequent handling of deaths and burials at workhouses in particular.

William Naddy (b. 1863), a farmer from Cill Mhic Sheain, Inistioge, County Kilkenny, recounted:

There was a fever hospital in Ballyrocksuist and a cholera house in the Mill Road. Patients were removed to the cholera house when there was no hope of their recovery. In some cases the patients were dead on admittance. They were buried in bottomless coffins in a large pit in the corner of the present graveyard. These coffins had hinges attached to the bottoms, a trigger was pulled and the body was let drop into the pit. Some clay was filled in over the body. Lime was then added. The corpse was buried without a habit, a sheet or anything available was wrapped over the body. Oftentimes this sheet or blanket was used again to cover a victim still living. The one coffin was known to have been used in the cholera house for more than twelve months. It was carried by two men like a hand-barrow, having handles front and rear. It is estimated that about three people in every house in the Inistioge district of the parish died either of fever or cholera during these years (qtd. in Póirtéir 117).

Naddy's account of a burial sheet placed on those still living is a disturbing truncation of the painstaking pre-Famine processes of vigilance over the dying, subsequent robing and positioning of the dead, and the placing of sheets at wakes. Not only did the rate of death accelerate as the demographic of victims expanded and the potential for customary burial diminished, the possibility of even dignity in death was ever-decreasing.

As, in a matter of a mere few years, hundreds of thousands died in the fever sheds of workhouses, or whilst trying to gain entrance to, or on ejectment from, workhouses, thousands more died in, or near, their own homes. A cruel twist on the familial sociality that defined pre-Famine death customs is revealed in an account written on a visit to a townland at Skibbereen, County Cork. A Cork magistrate, Nicholas Cummins, wrote in an open letter to the Duke of Wellington:

… In the first [hovel], six famished and ghastly skeletons, to all appearance dead, were huddled in a corner on some filthy straw, their sole covering what seemed a ragged horsecloth, their wretched legs hanging about, naked above the knees. I approached with horror and found by a low moaning they were alive – they were in fever, four children and a woman and what had once been a man. It is impossible to go through the detail. Suffice it to say that in a few minutes I was surrounded by at least 200 of such phantoms, such frightful spectres as no words can describe. By far the greater number were delirious, either from Famine or fever. Their demonic yells are still ringing in my ears and their horrible images are fixed upon my brain …. (qtd. in Foynes 52)

The full letter was published in *The Times* on December 24, 1846. Articles published in the *Cork Examiner* that month by a writer accompanying Dr Donovan on his harrowing rounds through the community bear further testimony to individuals dying among family members who themselves had insufficient physical energy to then bury any bodies or to even help each other (Foynes 51–2).

The appalling degradation of such death begot increasingly crude methods of burial, and many did not even receive the formality of a shared sheet or common coffin. Instead, corpses were piled onto animal-drawn carts, as illustrated in Henry Smith's image "The Famine in Ireland – Funeral at Skibbereen – From a Sketch by Mr H. Smith", published on January 30, 1847 in the *ILN* [Figure 9]. The illustration's frenzied action implies no funeral or farewell for these corpses destined for perfunctory entombment in Famine pits.

Across Cathal Póirtéir's selections for the NFC archive, a portrait of desperation emerges. Wheelbarrows and planks were used to convey bodies to burial sites, and some of the dead were buried on the way because men were too weak from starvation to carry bodies far. Others are reported as having had even less ceremony when people had to bury their relatives and neighbors at roadsides and in fields while on the move towards ports or in search of food, work, or housing relief. In some instances entire families died at roadsides and in ditches; their unburied bodies were later eaten by vermin. Others crawled into graves to await death in situ, anticipating that no one would bury them. Fear of contagion spreading from corpses was so unremitting across communities that it contributed both to hastened burials and possibly to the depletion of local knowledge regarding the locations of unmarked Famine burial sites. This is suggested by Dáithí Ó Ceanntabhail, a National teacher from Croom, County Limerick:

They were buried where they were found by opening the fence and shifting the poor corpse into the gap so formed. The ditch was then built over the body and some stones set into the bocastwork [sic] of the fence to mark the grave. The memory in later years of a Famine burial having been made at a certain point produced a superstitious fear in the minds of the people, a fear which had its origins I think, in the horrible dread of contagion which filled the survivors in an area where death mowed a wide swath (qtd. in Póirtéir 187).

Furthermore, the countrywide pressure for relief measures meant that some deaths were not necessarily acknowledged and, hence, left undocumented. The National Folklore Commission researcher and historian Seán O'Sullivan recounted an example at Tuosist, Kenmare, County Kerry: "One day Stephen Regan met a dog dragging a child's head along. He took the head from the dog and buried it and set a tree over it. The family to whom the child belonged were getting relief for the child and for that reason did not report the death" (qtd. in Póirtéir 187).

Figure 9 | Henry Smith, "The Famine in Ireland – Funeral at Skibbereen – from a Sketch by Mr H. Smith" (*Illustrated London News*, January 30, 1847)

FAMINE GRAVES, DARK TOURISM, AND SHARED MEMORY

Sustained campaigning, tireless research, and the much-tested enthusiasm of numerous individuals and local-interest groups throughout the island of Ireland have conserved a lot of what there is of the material memory of Famine burials. At the time of the one hundred and fiftieth anniversary of the Famine, the government of the Irish Republic made available limited funds to restore graveyards: £1,000 per graveyard was provided for their renovation in counties Antrim, Clare, Cork, Donegal, Kerry, Kildare, Leitrim, Longford, Meath, Monaghan, Tipperary, Waterford, and Wexford, while £5,000 apiece was contributed towards the funding of various local commemorations, such as memorials, maps, exhibitions, village renovations, and plays; this funding was in the context of wider nationally and internationally funded commemorative projects.[10] Following the establishment of the National Famine Commemoration Committee in 2008, it held its first annual national remembrance ceremony in 2009 at a memorialized Famine plot at Abbeystrewery Cemetery on the outskirts of Skibbereen, County Cork.

Many Famine graves across the island are as yet unidentified and, therefore, unacknowledged. A significant exception is St Mark's Famine Cemetery in Cashel, County Tipperary, where research by historian Martin Bob O'Dwyer and advocacy by locals resulted in a unique memorializing of a Famine burial site, which was made formally accessible in 2009. The cemetery is defined by a remarkable wall with over a thousand names of the Famine dead thought interred there; they are listed in an echo of the records of the Cashel workhouse entries, with dates of death, and names and ages of the dead.[11]

Typically, aside from those living locally, to visit the known Famine graveyards generally entails a considerable commitment to destination. The seeking out of less heralded Famine pits, particularly those located outside of cities or towns, requires an active form of tourism. Referencing R. J. Johnston's work, Greg Ringer writes that "destination [can] be understood ... as a phenomenon of personal experience" (5):

... both a psychological state of arrival and a process of spatial movement, as well as a culturally-defined geography of places, some clearly visible, others not, around which individuals construct and reconstruct ways of life that express "who they are and what is expected of them" (9).

Where Famine mass gravesites are enacted as destinations for remembrance of the past, the sites are affiliated with heritage tourism, both historic and cultural. In these places, as at the more conventionally signposted and memorialized burial sites, visitors can have a contemplative and immersive engagement with shared forms of remembrance, as with the solitary production of memory.

At the Clones Famine graveyard in County Monaghan, a rare figurative sculpture of an adult Famine corpse is a focal point of the site **[Figure 10]**. The vast majority of Famine memorial figurations depict living, though often barely living, adults, with occasional renderings of dead or dying infants. The ungendered body in Carolyn Mulholland's life-sized bronze sculpture (2001) is laid out in the rigor mortis of death and overlaid with a sculpted sheet. Given the setting, Mulholland presents the visitor with a displayed body as a spectacle, reminiscent of the laying out of the bodies of celebrated figures, such as politicians or religious leaders. But this is not a named or famous individual in a luxurious casket within a grand environment. Rather, the visitor finds themself at a somber outdoor wake, hosted at a site of unceremonious

Figure 10 | Carolyn Mulholland, Famine memorial, Famine graveyard, Clones, County Monaghan

interment. Myles Campbell observes: "By dispensing with the monumentality and heroism that characterize much historic Irish public sculpture, Mulholland creates figures who are often ordinary rather than extraordinary in their scale, allowing the viewer to interact with them in a more personal way" (249). The unsettlingly proximity by way of scale of the unnamed dead Famine victim of Mulholland's sculpture invites the visitor to consider those who died as individuals who, by dint of abominable circumstance, passed into the anonymity definitive of mass graves.

County Monaghan, along with its surrounding counties, was a densely populated area prior to the Famine, and – as in comparably well-populated rural areas throughout Ireland – was hard hit at this time. Mary Daly notes the population fell by 29.2 per cent between 1841 and 1851 (597). A memorial plaque at the Clones site includes this text (in capital letters):

> *Erected in memory of all*
> *the people from Clones Union*
> *who died because of*
> *the Great Famine 1845–1850*
> *Also those who died*
> *in the workhouse 1845–1921*
> *The meek shall inherit the earth*
> *PS 37.11*

In 2011 Clones was the site of the annual National Famine Commemoration ceremony. As sites of mass burial, with no individual grave markers, Famine plots are transformed into cemeteries for remembrance when visually and materially marked by various memorial forms, such as commemorative gatherings and the syntax of landscaping. The area surrounding Mulholland's sculpture is clearly monumentalized, with curved walls and various memorial elements echoing international languages of cemetery and monumental formalism, against which both the anonymity and singularity unpinning Mulholland's dignified corpse is emphasized.[12] This approach is countered at other sites by explicit associations with celebrated individuals.

Swinford workhouse was built in the early 1840s, but only admitted its first inmates during 1846. The Famine burial plot is at the back of what is now a working hospital [Figure 11]. The site has strong associations with Michael Davitt, who in a speech in London in 1890, "Defence of the Land League", recalled his mother's memories of Swinford workhouse:

I remember hearing from her a graphic account of how 300 poor people who had died of starvation round about where I was born, between Straide and Swinford, had been thrown into one pit in the corner of the workhouse yard, without coffin, without sermon, without anything which denotes respect for the dead (qtd. in Delaney & Mac Suibhne 6).

Figure 11 | Workhouse and Famine graveyard, Swinford, County Mayo

Davitt was born in nearby Straide, where his family suffered such poverty that he and his mother attempted entry to the workhouse. He then grew up in Lancashire, later returned to Ireland, was a founder of the Land League – an agrarian protest movement – and became a Member of Parliament. An entrance stone to the Swinford graveyard states (in capital letters):

> *Erected*
> *by the people of Swinford*
> *to the memory of*
> *564 Famine victims*
> *buried in this place.*
> *May they rest in peace.*

The graveyard is a large field with a centrally placed headstone memorial. The headstone has etched portraits of Michael Davitt and Mahatma Gandhi. Beside each is a short quotation. The rest of the text links the hundreds buried here to Davitt's founding of the Land League and ongoing struggles for "a just and equitable world".

Similar double links to local historic figures and international humanitarians are found at other Famine gravesites. For example, at Callan Famine graveyard in Baunta Commons, County Kilkenny, text on a memorial entrance stone to the site draws attention to the one hundred and fiftieth anniversary of the death of local man Fr Edmund Rice, who founded the Christian Brothers in Ireland, and also quotes social scientist Dessalegn Rahmato. Also at Callan – a haunting and beautifully preserved out-of-the-way workhouse and Famine gravesite – the Irish Famine is listed in the context of a series of humanitarian disasters across the world. This, and imagery evoking a universal figure of human suffering, are in keeping with the advocacy interests of the NGO Afri (Action from Ireland), which commissioned the memorial.

Though Swinford Graveyard is in close proximity to the former workhouse, it is, like Callan, defined by the shaping of its natural environment: a perimeter wall, a line of tall trees, and maintained short grass. The relatively modest headstone accentuates the scale of the site and the historic function of the ground beneath. The typically personal ritual of mourning the loss of a life, as occurs on visiting a cemetery, is at a site such as this powerfully linked, through the awareness of landscape, to the magnitude of historical experience. Though presented as a designated and sheltered space for mourning – much as any cemetery is – this site's relative emptiness and minimal signs promote reflection on what remains underfoot: the ultimate witnesses now collectively absent.

On the roadside outside the town of Macroom, County Cork is an iron gateway to a path through a field. This leads to a walled area by tall trees. On the stone slabs at the entrance gate to Carrigastira Graveyard is engraved unattributed text and the date 1846–47:

> *Our pen, our art won fame:*
> *Philosophers to Ireland came*
> *Alas came penal laws, tyrant's hand,*
> *Famine, plague stalked our land*
> *By yonder plot in mass we lay,*
> *Pilgrim, reflect, and pray.*
> *May this land at peace and free*
> *Again serve God and humanity.*

The graveyard is characterized by dense undergrowth in parts and rough ground throughout, with large intermittent stones and some cleared areas **[Figure 12]**. There is a set of cut logs arranged for a group to sit on, signs – "Mass Grave" and "Perimeter Walk" – and a chapel-like hut. These man-made and constructed interventions cultivate, by counterpoint, the site's air of untamed nature. The canopies of trees and tall bushes create a sense of interiority and differentiate the site from the surrounding open countryside. Attempts to walk it are greatly thwarted by tangles of undergrowth and very bumpy terrain. The graveyard was used to bury inmates from Macroom workhouse.

As a memorialized Famine burial site, Carrigastira represents a meeting point of the unmarked, and many unknown, burial locations with the more formalized range of extant graveyards and cemeteries. These deeply affecting sites provide spaces

Figure 12 | Carrigastira Famine graveyard, County Cork

for remembrance of the horrors and scale of Famine death and burial, informed by the visual and textual discourses of national, local, and folk historical practices, as indicated differentially at each site. They are also implicit in transnational modes of so-called dark tourism: tourism of sites associated with death.

Geoffrey M. White notes that tourism practices "recreate a social milieu in which the past is interactively represented, understood and evaluated in relation to multiple, and at times competing, frames of history" (76). Writing on the "tourism memoryscape" of what he calls "war tourism", his analyses relate specifically to group tours at sites of conflict. At a connected social level of dark tourism, Philip Stone suggests shades of darkness to distinguish such sites, as associated with death more broadly. The darkest types of sites are "Sites of Death and Suffering", while at the lighter end of the chart are "Sites Associated with Suffering and Death" (151). The first type has "higher political influence and ideology" with "an education orientation and location authenticity", while the second has "lower political influence and ideology, entertainment orientation and non-location authenticity" (151).

By Stone's assessment, off-site representations or memorials form the "lighter" side when posited against "darker" sites typically tied to visible evidence and thus implied historical certainty. This is borne out in studies on visual commemorative cultures around death associated with different grievous histories, exemplified in Peter Hohenhaus's discussion on what he calls "place authenticity" in qualifying visitor experiences at memorial sites to the Rwandan Genocide. However, the gap between reality (darkness) and representation (light) is more nuanced when some level of mediation is recognized as part of the designation of any site commemorating a grievous history. In his analysis of concentration camps as memorial sites, Chris Keil has elucidated on this as "the artful and conscious construction of illusion" (490). In commemorations of Famine-era death and burial, overlaps between "place authenticity" and representation are not only apparent but made meaningful at an overtly hybrid site: one that is both a burial ground and a garden.

Figure 13 | Famine Garden of Remembrance, Carrick-on-Shannon, County Leitrim

The Famine Garden of Remembrance at Carrick-on-Shannon, County Leitrim is located behind the former workhouse in the town **[Figure 13]**. James H. Tuke, a Quaker, who visited in 1846, wrote:

I have already stated that owing to the want of funds, great difficulty exists in many Unions in providing for inmates. The worst which I visited was that of Carrick-on-Shannon (which opened in 1842); it is in a miserable state and the doors were closed against further admission; and although built for 700 had but 280 inmates; gates were besieged by seventy or eighty wretched beings who in vain implores for admission. Numbers of them were in various stage of fever, which was terribly prevalent in the neighbourhood, and the fever-shed was overcrowded. Two months before my visit, the doors of the workhouse were opened and the inmates expelled entailing upon them the most dire misery (qtd. in O'Connor 123).

The workhouse is since home to St Patrick's Community Hospital. An attic is preserved as a reminder of the building's past, and has on permanent display an artwork on the Famine by Irish artist Alanna O'Kelly. According to Donal O'Grady, the workhouse graveyard was opened, in 1849, because local graveyards could not cope with the number of burials (*Leitrim Observer*, September 12, 2008).

With seating, a water feature, soft grass, and a selection of native Irish trees, the garden is tranquil. The distressing scenes it would have featured in Famine times – the hasty burial of the putrid, bloated, and skeletal bodies – seems overwritten by the contemplative atmosphere. Though a plaque reminds visitors of the site's former use, the site is likely used by hospital workers and visitors as a place to relax. Given both its location in the town and its beautification, unlike many mass Famine gravesites, this one has a dual purpose: a garden that is not only for remembrance but is also an element of ongoing, everyday life in the town.

BELATED WITNESSING: REPRESENTATIONS OF FAMINE DEATH AND BURIAL

The amalgamation of commemorative and leisure purposes that defines gardens of remembrance is a characteristic shared by memorial parks. In Galway city, between the picturesque inlet at the Claddagh and the Atlantic splendor of the seafront promenade at Salthill, lies the Celia Griffin Memorial Park, near Grattan beach **[Figure 14]**.

In March 1847 an inquest was held in Galway following the death of a young girl at a convent in the city:

An inquest was held on Thursday last, before Michael Perrin, Esq., D.C., at the Presentation Convent, on view of the body of Celia Griffin, a girl about six years of age, from the village of Corindulla, near Ross, in this county. It appeared in evidence that the poor creature had been reduced to extreme poverty and that the family to whom she belonged, eight in number, were in the same pitiful condition. She had been recommended to the Ladies of the Presentation, by Rev. George Usher, as a fit object for relief, and accordingly she and her two sisters received a daily breakfast at that excellent Institute. They met Mr Usher on the Rahoon road about a fortnight ago, but Famine had so preyed upon her feeble constitution, that, on the morning of Wednesday, she was unable to taste food of any description – so that on the post mortem examination made by Doctor Staunton, there was not a particle found in her stomach.

She with her father, mother, brothers, and sisters, came to Galway about six weeks ago, in the hope of obtaining some charitable relief, and during that period have been begging in the streets, and about the country. The parents of the deceased formerly resided on the estate of Thomas Martin, Esq, MP. When Doctor Staunton was called on he found deceased in a state of inanition, except an occasional convulsive action of the muscles, and her body might be said to be literally skin and bone – with all the appearance of starvation. She was so exhausted, as not to be able to use the food supplied to her. The Jury found that her death was caused for want of the common necessaries of life, before she received relief at the Presentation Convent.

This text, headed "Starvation Inquest", is presented on a stone panel near the roadside entrance to the memorial park. At the foot of the stone it reads: "This park is named in memory of Celia Griffin and all the children who suffered and died in the Great Famine".

Further in, set against a view of the hills of County Clare across Galway Bay, is a circular paved monument area featuring three upright stoneworks in a formation reminiscent of ancient standing stones. Text on the Mutton Light Famine Memorial outlines its dedication:

> *This memorial is dedicated*
> *to the captains and crews*
> *who carried many*
> *thousands of victims of the*
> *Great Famine to safety*
> *1847–1853*
> *It bears the names of*
> *one hundred of their ships*
> *Deo Gratia*

The memorial's name refers to the lighthouse on Mutton Island, which would have shed a final beam of light from Ireland for the thousands who emigrated from Galway's port as a result of the Famine.

With no figuration, Celia Griffin is recalled by the naming of the park and the reproduction of text from the report of the inquest into her death. It is likely that, as reflected across the NFC archive, fear of contagion may have prevented the citizens of Galway from being more helpful in her hour of dire need. However, in prolonged deprived conditions of famine, anti-social behavior and extreme breakdowns of familial relations can also arise. Instances are described in Famine witness accounts across the archive of the NFC, and borne out by statistical analyses. For example,

Figure 14 | Celia Griffin Memorial Park, Galway

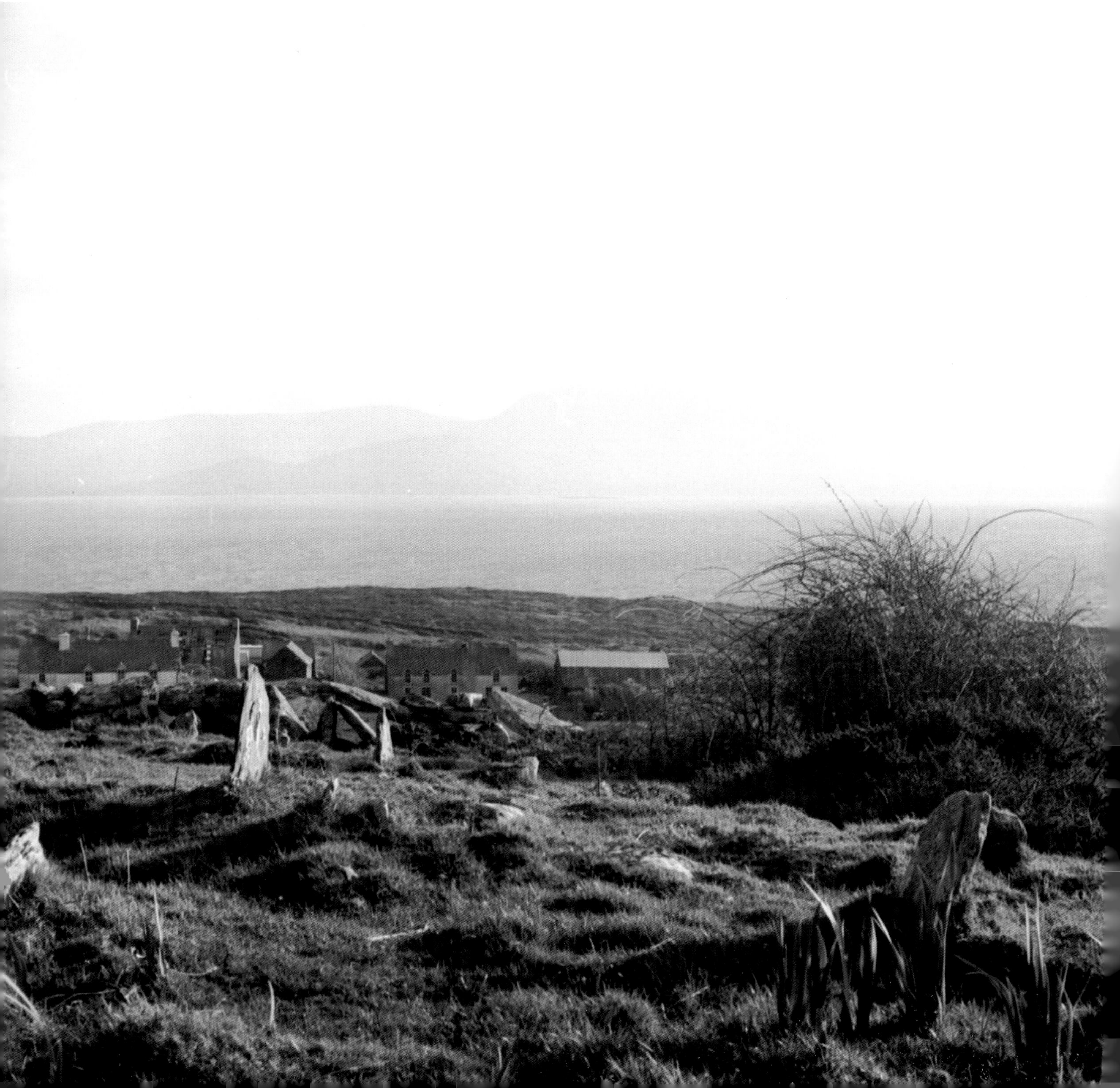

Dr Donovan noted a fatal struggle between a father and son, and described mothers snatching food from the hands of their children (cited in Crawford 202), and in the late 1840s the incidences of burglary and robbery increased fivefold (Ó Gráda 53).

The Celia Griffin Memorial Park focus on the singular death of a young person as implicitly emblematic of the broad grievous history that decided many fates is an approach common to the wider international landscape of commemorative forms. Narratives and motifs of young girls are particularly resonant, as exemplified by the publication of Anne Frank's diary, the film that tells her story, and the house museum to her memory. While the central material elements of the memorial in the Celia Griffin Memorial Park emphasizes a more broadly positive narrative of a sort of survival by way of emigration than suggested by the park's titular focus, the spacious location, defined by the panorama of the sea, creates a representation of history that is nonetheless geographically rooted at the edge of a landmass. Set across from a housing area, the area is a popular walking route along the coastline, so creating an actively populated space for commemoration, both solitary and social.

The western coastal landscape of Ireland also features in visual representations that document Famine burial, including documentary photography and art installation. The caption of a photograph taken by Séamas Mac Philib, "View of Gort na Cille Graveyard. Unbaptised children and Famine victims reputedly buried here. Kilcrohane, Bantry, County Cork (1977)", indicates uncertain knowledge about this site **[Figure 15]**. It also points to an aspect of Irish burial history that preceded and continued after the Famine. Stillborn and unbaptized children were regularly buried outside of church or consecrated grounds in plots known as *cillíní* (*cillín* is Irish for "little cell" or "little churchyard", and a commonly used term for children's burial grounds). Eileen M. Murphy notes evidence that while the Church regarded these sites as marginal, close family members of the dead treated them as important (409). She outlines attempts to replicate funerary practices in the choice of these burial sites: places were chosen that had previous ecclesiastical associations or were on unusable land that would not later be disturbed. Her study also indicates that subtle internal demarcations were made on these sites, such as configurations of stones, the conspicuousness of white quartz, and even figurations, and, further, that these modestly memorializing interventions suggest return visits and sustained mourning.

During Famine times some of these sites, as pictured by Mac Philib, became Famine graves also. Mac Philib's image is from the NFC's collection of photographs of marked and unmarked burial sites within its wider collection of eighty thousand images. Despite having limited photographic equipment (Briody 245–6), the photographic archive was begun in the 1940s by Kevin Danaher, who was employed as a collector since 1939 (Briody 336–7). Danaher compiled and cataloged his "extensive photographic documentation of traditional life" (Mac Philib 153), as well as instigating the questionnaire format used for many of the informant interviews in the archive. Other researchers contributed images, such as this one by historian Mac

Figure 15 | "View of Gort na Cille Graveyard. Unbaptised children and Famine victims reputedly buried here. Kilcrohane, Bantry, County Cork (1977)"

Philib. In the foreground the graveyard is demarcated by stones roughly jutting out at various angles from an uneven ground. The romantic tonality of the black-and-white image augments the depth of field, distancing the misty mountains on the far side of the bay, as the beauty of the scene seems to aesthetically trace the unstable relativities of historical understanding.

At a beach known as Teampall Dumach Mhór (Church of the Great Sandbank) at Thallabawn, County Mayo, there was a mound of earth, rocks, and bones. It was the location of a sixth-century monastic settlement, and later became a Famine burial site. Thallabawn is an anglicized version of the Irish *Tallamh Bhan*, meaning "white ground". The area was "known as a sanctuary to 17th century map makers and was referred to as the Wastelands by local people in the 19th and 20th century" (IMMA). The mound's erosion by the sea was underway as O'Kelly was recording the site for her audio-visual art installation *Sanctuary/Wasteland* (1994) **[Figure 16]**.

In the installation, a series of detailed images and details are projected onto visual sequences of the mound, landscape, and dwellings from that coastal region. The work's dark hues, disconcertingly low keening sounds, and cyclical format, along with its double title, reflect on the complexity of comprehending place or history in any final sense. O'Kelly learned how to keen for this and other performance works, and in *Sanctuary/Wasteland* she proceeds to sing a lament in Irish (Marshall 19). In its initial form of a slide/audio-tape installation, *Sanctuary/Wasteland* was exhibited in *Representations of the Famine* in 1999. Curated by Catherine Marshall at the Irish Museum of Modern Art (IMMA), Dublin, this was a rare exhibition of Famine commemorative visual culture, and was comprised of both artworks contemporary to the 1990s and historical paintings and illustrations from various collections.

In a 2001 public lecture at IMMA, O'Kelly noted that, as a child growing up in County Wexford, she had heard stories about a local field left fallow where Famine dead were said to be buried. This, along with other personal, artistic, and research experiences, informed her interest in making a series of works on the subject of the Famine, of which *Sanctuary/Wasteland* is one. Documenting the site at Thallabawn through her art practice, O'Kelly extends the possibility for remembrances of Famine-era burials otherwise left to be eroded from social memory by the energetic forces of both nature and cultural continuance.

A belated witnessing to an outcome of Famine death, impersonal burial, *Sanctuary/Wasteland* functions as an after-image of an expansive grievous history. It is a history in which the passing of individual lives were swept up and rendered statistical by the enormity of suffering. The devastation of disease, the rate and types of death, and fears of contagion not only curtailed practices of mourning and burial during the calamitous height of the Famine but have also shaped the Famine's visual commemorative forms and related ongoing patterns of remembrance.

Figure 16 | Alanna O'Kelly, *Sanctuary/Wasteland* [Detail]

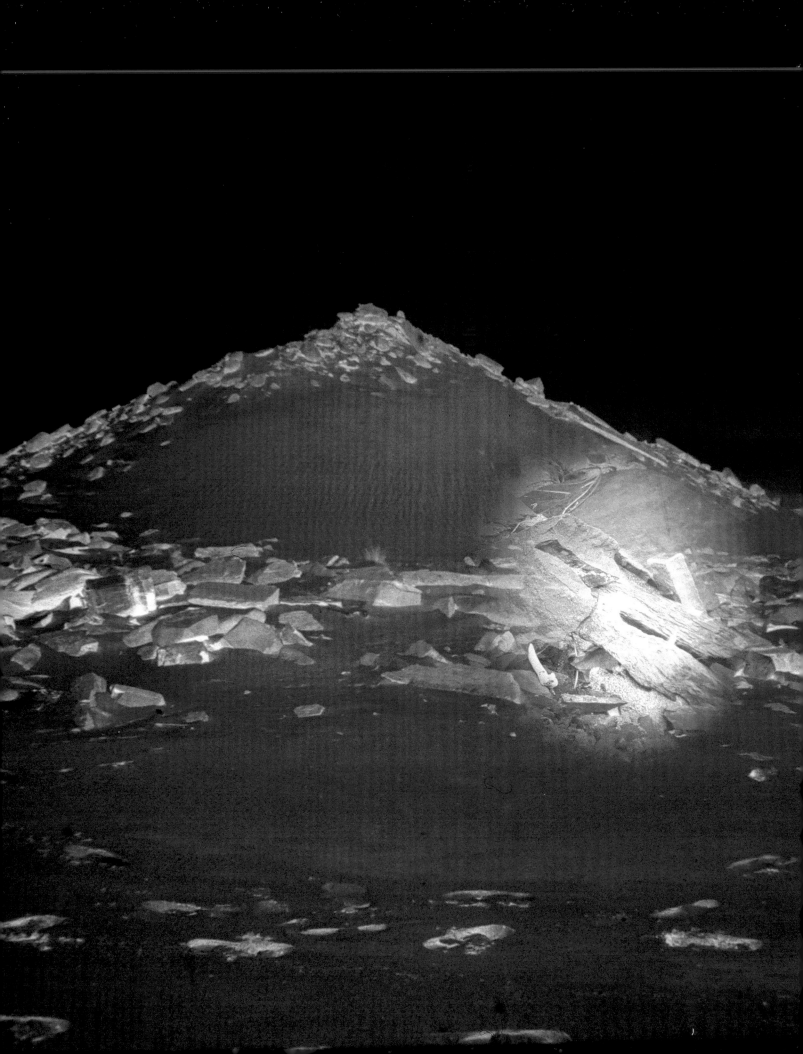

ENDNOTES

[1] Wicklow-born Davidson traveled abroad frequently, and exhibited regularly at the Watercolour Society and the Royal Hibernian Academy in Dublin.

[2] Susie Linfield uses the term to describe experiences of "defeat and atrocity" (xiv).

[3] From an artisan background, Grogan spent some years in America, then returned to Cork, where he made a living as a landscape artist, book illustrator, and art teacher.

[4] The fascinating complexities of this famous example are discussed in detail by Lysaght ("Caoineadh os coinn coirp") and Ó Coileáin.

[5] Burton studied art in Dublin and exhibited regularly in Ireland and Dublin, and was popular as a portraitist. Burton stopped painting when he became director of the National Gallery in London for twenty years from 1874.

[6] Two years later Macdonald moved to London, where he achieved moderate academic success, exhibiting at the British Institute and the Royal Hibernian Academy, Dublin (Murray 178). In 1847 he exhibited in London his painting *The Discovery of the Potato Blight*, now housed at University College, Dublin.

[7] Belfast-born Brandt spent most of her life in Dublin, was a member of the Royal Hibernian Academy, a professional portraitist, and a governor of the National Gallery of Ireland.

[8] Cristín Leach, "Muriel Brandt's 1916 Breadline", *Sunday Times* (Ireland), March 17, 2016.

[9] Discussed in O'Sullivan, *The Tombs of a Departed Race*, 25–6.

[10] Dáil Éireann, vol. 477, 26 March, 1997. All currency is in Irish pounds (*punt*), the national currency of the time.

[11] Carved by stonemason Brendan O'Riordan.

[12] Mulholland proposed that her sculpture would lie in greater isolation on the site, on a low bier-like platform (Mark-Fitzgerald 123–4).

WORKS CITED

Agamben, Giorgio. *Remnants of Auschwitz*. New York: Zone Books, 2008.

Apel, Dora. *Memory Effects: The Holocaust and the Art of Secondary Witnessing*. New Brunswick, New Jersey and London: Rutgers University Press, 2002.

Bartlett, Thomas. *Ireland: A History.* Cambridge: Cambridge University Press, 2010.

Bourke, Angela. *The Burning of Bridget Cleary: A True Story*. London: Random House, 2010.

---. "Inner lives: creativity and survival in Irish rural life". *Éire-Ireland* 46.3–4 (2011).

Bourke, Marie. "200th anniversary of Frederic William Burton, 1816–1900". *History Ireland* 24.1 (2016).

Briody, Mícheál, *The Irish Folklore Commission: 1935–1970: History, Ideology, Methodology*. Helsinki: Finnish Literature Society, 2008.

Cahill, Katherine. "In the mainstream of Irish naturalism: the art of Lilian Lucy Davidson". *Irish Arts Review Yearbook* 15 (1999).

Campbell, Myles. "Carolyn Mulholland". *Art and Architecture of Ireland Volume III: Sculpture 1600–2000*. Eds. Andrew Carpenter and Paula Murphy. Dublin: Royal Irish Academy, 2015.

Campbell, Stephen J. *The Great Irish Famine: Words, and Images from the Famine Museum, Strokestown Park, County Roscommon*. Roscommon: Famine Museum, 1994.

Corrigan Correll, Timothy. "Believers, sceptics, and charlatans: evidential rhetoric, the fairies, and fairy healers in Irish oral narrative and belief". *Folklore* 116 (2005).

Crawford, Margaret E. "Subsistence crises and famines in Ireland: a nutritionist's view". *Famine: The Irish Experience, 900–1900*. Ed. Margaret E. Crawford. Edinburgh: John Donald Publishers, 1989.

Daly, Mary. "Historians and the Famine: a beleaguered species?" *Irish Historical Studies* 30.120 (1997).

Delany, Enda and Breandán Mac Suibhne. "Editors' introduction: 'To asses even the animal's right of existence'". *Ireland's Great Famine and Popular Politics*. Eds. Enda Delany and Breandán Mac Suibhne. New York and Oxon: Routledge, 2016.

Dunne, Tom. "Painters on the margins". *Irish Arts Review* 29.1 (2012).

Figgis, Nicola. "Nathaniel Grogan". *Art and Architecture of Ireland Volume II: Painting 1600–1900*. Eds. Andrew Carpenter, Nicola Figgis, Maria Arnold, Nesta Butler, and Elizabeth Mayes. Dublin: Royal Irish Academy, 2015.

Foynes, Peter. *The Great Famine in Skibbereen and District.* Skibbereen: Irish Famine Commemoration (Skibbereen Ltd), 2004.

Geary, Laurence M. "'The late disastrous epidemic': medical relief and the Great Famine". *Fearful Realities: New Perspectives on the Famine*. Eds. Chris Morash and Richard Hayes. Dublin: Irish Academic Press, 1996.

Hallam, Elizabeth and Jenny Hockey. *Death, Memory, and Material Culture.* Oxford and New York: Berg, 2001.

Hirsch, Marianne. "Projected memory: Holocaust photographs in personal and public fantasy". *Acts of Memory: Cultural Recall in the Present.* Eds. Mieke Bal, Jonathon Crewe, and Leo Spitzer. Hanover, NH: University Press of New England, 1999.

Hohenhaus, Peter. "Commemorating and commodifying the Rwandan Genocide". *Dark Tourism and Place Identity: Managing and Interpreting Dark Places*. Eds. Leanne White and Elspeth Frew. London and New York: Routledge, 2013.

Irish Museum of Modern Art. "Súil Eile: selected works from the IMMA collection at Ballina Arts Centre, Co Mayo". Press release, 2007.

Johnston, R. J. *A Question of Place: Exploring the Practice of Human Geography*. Oxford and Cambridge, MA: Blackwell, 1991.

Keil, Chris. "Sightseeing in the mansions of the dead". *Social and Cultural Geography* 6.4 (2005).

Kennedy, Brian P. *Irish Painting*. Dublin: Town House and Country House, 1993.

Kinealy, Christine. *The Great Irish Famine: Impact, Ideology and Rebellion*. Basingstoke and New York: Palgrave 2002.

Kinmonth, Claudia. *Irish Rural Interiors in Art*. New Haven, CT and London: Yale University Press, 2006.

Leach, Cristín. "Muriel Brandt's 1916 Breadline". *Sunday Times* (Ireland). March 17, 2016.

Linfield, Susie. *The Cruel Radiance: Photography and Political Violence*. Chicago and London: Chicago University Press, 2012.

Lysaght, Patricia. "Caoineadh os coinn coirp: the lament for the dead in Ireland". *Folklore* 108 (1997).

---. "Hospitality at wakes and funerals in Ireland from the seventeenth to the nineteenth century: some evidence from the written record". *Folklore* 114 (2003).

---. "The banshee". *Death and the Irish: A Miscellany*. Ed. Salvador Ryan. Dublin: Wordwell, 2016.

Mac Philib, Seamas. "Obituaries: Kevin Danaher (Caoimhín Ó Danachair)". *Journal of the Royal Society of Antiquaries of Ireland* 132 (2002).

Mark-Fitzgerald, Emily. *Commemorating the Irish Famine: Memory and the Monument*. Liverpool: Liverpool University Press, 2013.

Marshall, Catherine. *Monuments and Memorials of the Great Famine*. Hamden, CT: Quinnipiac University Press, 2014.

Martin, James Gerard, "The Society of the St. Vincent de Paul as an emerging social phenomenon in mid-nineteenth century Ireland". MA thesis, National College of Industrial Relations, 1993.

Murphy, Eileen M. "Children's burial grounds in Ireland (*cillíní*) and parental emotions toward infant death". *International Journal of History & Archaeology* 15 (2011).

Murray, Peter. *Illustrated Summary Catalogue of the Crawford Municipal Art Gallery*. Cork: City of Cork VEC, 1992.

Ó Ciosáin, Niall. "Approaching a folklore archive: the Irish Folklore Commission and the memory of the Great Famine". *Folklore* 115 (2004).

Ó Coileáin, Seán. "The Irish lament: an oral genre". *Studia Hibernica* 24 (1988).

O'Connor, John. *The Workhouses of Ireland: The Fate of Ireland's Poor.* Dublin: Anvil Books, 1995.

O Crualaoich, Gearóid. "The merry wake". In *Irish Popular Culture 1650–1850*. Eds. James S. Donnelly Jr. and Kerby A. Miller. Dublin: Irish Academic Press, 1998.

Ó Gráda, Cormac. *Famine: A Short History*. Princeton, NJ and Oxford: Princeton University Press, 2009.

O'Grady, Donal. "Carrick workhouse attic memorial opened". *Leitrim Observer*, September 12, 2008.

O'Kelly, Alanna. "Winter lecture". Irish Museum of Modern Art (IMMA), December 4, 2001; audio courtesy of Irish Museum of Modern Art.

Ó Murchadha, Ciarán. *The Great Famine: Ireland's Agony, 1845–1852*. London and New York: Continuum, 2011.

O'Rourke, John. *On a Cross*. Pamphlet, *c*. 1885, no place of publication.

Ó Súilleabháin, Seán. *Irish Folk Custom and Belief.* Dublin: Mercier Press, 1967.

O'Sullivan, Niamh. *The Tombs of a Departed Race: Illustrations of Ireland's Great Hunger*. Hamden, CT: Quinnipiac University Press, 2014.

---. *In the Lion's Den: Daniel Macdonald, Ireland, and Empire*. Hamden, CT: Quinnipiac University Press, 2016.

Póirtéir, Cathal. *Famine Echoes*. Dublin: Gill & Macmillan, 1995.

Rieff, David. *Against Remembrance*. Dublin: Liffey Press, 2011.

Rigney, Ann. "Plentitude, scarcity, and the circulation of cultural memory". *Journal of European Studies* 35.1 (2005).

Ringer, Greg. "Introduction". *Destinations: Cultural Landscapes of Tourism*. Ed. Greg Ringer. London and New York: Routledge, 2005.

Stone, Philip R. "A dark tourism spectrum: towards a typology of death and macabre related tourist sites, attractions, and exhibitions." *Tourism* 54.2 (2006).

White, Geoffrey M. "Is Paris burning? Touring America's 'good war' in France". *History & Memory* 27.2 (2015).

Young, James. *At Memory's Edge: After-images of the Holocaust in Contemporary Art and Architecture.* New Haven, CT and London: Yale University Press, 2000.

IMAGES

Cover

(Henry) Mark Anthony
1817–86
Sunset (View of the Rock of Cashel from the Village)
Oil on canvas
51 x 51 in (129.5 x 129.5 cm)
Image provided by Ireland's Great Hunger Museum, Quinnipiac University

Figure 1

Muriel Brandt
1909–81
An Gorta
c. 1946
Oil on canvas
Image provided by National Museum of Ireland
© 2017 Artists Rights Society, New York/IVARO, Dublin

Figure 2

Lilian Lucy Davidson
1879–1954
Gorta
1946
Previously known as *Burying the Child*
Oil on canvas
27.5 x 35.5 in (70 x 90 cm)
© Estate of Lilian Lucy Davidson
Image provided by Ireland's Great Hunger Museum, Quinnipiac University

Figure 3

Nathaniel Grogan the Elder
1740–1807
The Wake
c. 1783
Oil on panel
18.5 x 24.5 in (47 x 62.2 cm)
Gift of the Martin I. and Margaret J. Zankel Revocable Trust and of the West Family Trust to the Fine Arts Museums Foundation
Image provided by the Fine Arts Museums of San Francisco

Figure 4

Frederic William Burton
1816–1900
The Aran Fisherman's Drowned Child
1841
Watercolour on paper
34.8 x 30.9 in (88.4 x 78.5 cm)
National Gallery of Ireland Collection, NGI.6048
Photo © National Gallery of Ireland

Figure 5

Daniel Macdonald
1820–53
Returning from an Irish Funeral
1842
Pen and ink on paper
22.5 x 27.3 in (57 x 69 cm)
Image provided by Ireland's Great Hunger Museum, Quinnipiac University

Figure 6

Muriel Brandt
1909–81
An Gorta [Detail]
c. 1946
Oil on canvas
Image provided by National Museum of Ireland
© 2017 Artists Rights Society, New York/IVARO, Dublin

Figure 7

James Mahony
1810–59
"Funeral at Shepperton Lakes"
Illustrated London News
February 13, 1847
Image provided by Ireland's Great Hunger Museum, Quinnipiac University

Figure 8

Famine Era Coffin Cross. Text purportedly written by Dr Thomas Willis
Presentation Sisters, St Anne's Retreat and Conference Centre, Killenard, Portarlington, County Laois
Image provided by author

Figure 9

Henry Smith
"The Famine in Ireland – Funeral at Skibbereen – from a Sketch by Mr H. Smith"
Illustrated London News
January 30, 1847
Image provided by Ireland's Great Hunger Museum, Quinnipiac University

Figure 10

Carolyn Mulholland
Famine memorial, Famine graveyard, Clones, County Monaghan
2001
Bronze
Photograph by Geri Kelly
© Carolyn Mullholland

Figure 11

Swinford Famine plot. Mass Famine grave, Swinford, County Mayo
Image provided by author

Figure 12

Carrigastira Famine graveyard, County Cork
Image provided by author

Figure 13

Famine Garden of Remembrance, Carrick-on-Shannon, County Leitrim
Image provided by author

Figure 14

Celia Griffin Memorial Park, Galway
Image provided by Des Kelly

Figure 15

"View of Gort na Cille Graveyard. Unbaptised children and Famine victims reputedly buried here. Kilcrohane, Bantry, County Cork (1977)"
Photograph by Séamas Mac Philib
© National Folklore Collection, UCD

Figure 16

Alanna O'Kelly
b. 1955
Sanctuary/Wasteland
1994
Video still
Image provided by Irish Museum of Modern Art
© Alanna O'Kelly

ACKNOWLEDGMENTS

Many thanks to the following for generously sharing research, knowledge, and expertise: Mary Ann Bolger, Michael Kenny, Niamh O'Sullivan, Catherine Marshall, Bernard Minogue, and Sr Alphonsus PBVM.

ABOUT THE AUTHOR

Niamh Ann Kelly lectures on the history of art and contemporary visual culture at the Dublin School of Creative Arts, Dublin Institute of Technology (DIT), Ireland. Her research interests are contemporary art, commemorative visual cultures of art, journalism, and museum and heritage practice, with a focus on visual, material, and spatial memorialization of grievous histories.

She has contributed to numerous publications, including *Art and Architecture of Ireland, Volume V: The Twentieth Century* (Dublin: Royal Irish Academy, 2014), Art and Architecture of Ireland, Volume III: Sculpture (Dublin: Royal Irish Academy, 2014), *Memory Ireland, Volume III: Cruxes in Irish Cultural Memory: The Famine and the Troubles* (Syracuse, NY: Syracuse University Press, 2014), *Art and Visibility in Migratory Culture: Conflict, Resistance, and Agency* (Amsterdam/New York: Rodopi, 2011), *Ireland's Great Hunger, Volume 2* (Lanham, MD/Boulder, CO/New York/Toronto/Plymouth (UK): University Press of America, 2010), *Representation Matters: (Re)Articulating Collective Identities in a Postcolonial World* (Amsterdam/New York: Rodopi 2010), *What is_Installation Art?* (Dublin: Irish Museum of Modern Art, 2010), and *Hugh Lane: Founder of a Gallery of Modern Art for Ireland* (London: Scala, 2008).

Her book *Imaging the Great Irish Famine: Representing Dispossession in Visual Culture* (London: I. B. Tauris) is due for publication in 2017.

IRELAND'S GREAT HUNGER MUSEUM | QUINNIPIAC UNIVERSITY PRESS ©2017

SERIES EDITOR

Niamh O'Sullivan

IMAGE RESEARCH

Claire Puzarne

DESIGN

www.rachelfoleydesigns.com

ACKNOWLEDGMENT

Office of Public Affairs, Quinnipiac University

PUBLISHER

Quinnipiac University Press

PRINTING

GRAPHYCEMS

ISBN 978-0-9978374-6-9

Ireland's Great Hunger Museum
Quinnipiac University

3011 Whitney Avenue
Hamden, CT 06518-1908
203-582-6500

www.ighm.org